"Sunny's Shifts His Brain: Teaching Children How to Use Their Brain to Change Their Behavior"

© 2014 YouthLight, Inc.
PO Box 115
Chapin, SC 29036
800-209-9774
www.youthlight.com

Cover Artwork and Illustrations by: Maja Sommersted

ISBN: 978-1-59850-161-2
Library of Congress Control Number: 2014940809

10 9 8 7 6 5 4 3 2 1
Printed in the United States

Hi there. My name is Sunny.
I like it when people say "Hi" to me.

Say, "Hi Sunny!"

Thanks, that makes me feel good.

Today I'm going to teach you how important your brain is and two ways to use your brain that will help you to think better and make better choices.

1. **CHECK**

2. **CRISSCROSS** and **SHIFT**

First, let's talk about our brain. Can we open up our head, look inside, and see our brain?

NO, but if we could...
It would be soft, squishy, gray with wrinkles, and jiggly like jelly!

Did you know that our brain is an organ? What is an organ?* What are some other organs we have in our body? Some organs can be replaced. We call that a transplant.

Can our brain be replaced? NO!

Can we go to the store and buy a new brain?

NOOOO!

This is the only brain we have. So, we need to take care of it!

I want to take care of my brain.
I'm sure you want to take care of your brain too.

What does our brain do for us?

It helps us...

think,

speak,

move,

and breathe.

It helps our heart beat

and much, much more.

In fact, our brain does EVERYTHING for us.
Absolutely EVERYTHING!

OH MY...

What would happen if we didn't have a brain?

We wouldn't be alive!

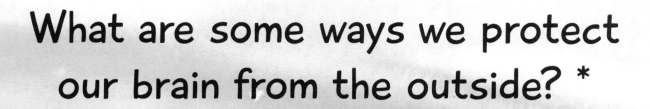

What are some ways we protect
our brain from the outside? *

Like wearing helmets.
What else?

What are some ways we protect our brain from the inside? *

Like eating healthy.
What else?

I have a couple more ideas about protecting our brain.
Here, let me explain. Our brain actually fires off with

ELECTRICITY

My brain is always firing off with

ELECTRICITY

every time I think. And I do want to think........a lot.

When our brain fires off, it sends messages through the brain stem and on down through our spinal column.

The messages even go to the tips of our fingers and toes, telling our body to move, breathe, speak, respond, feel, think, etc.

Our brain is so amazing! It has many complicated areas. But I'm going to share with you just two areas of our brain. That makes it simple.

We will call these two areas:
- The back of the brain
- The front of the brain

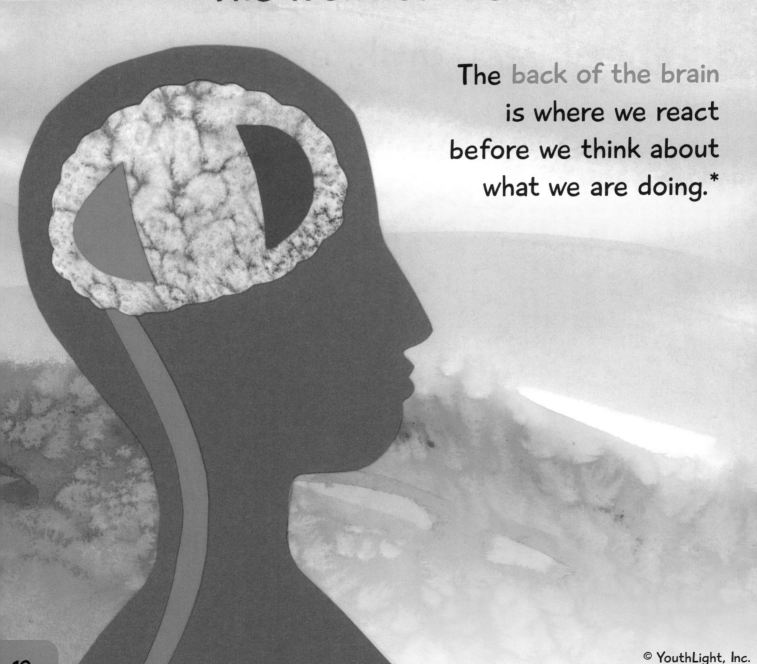

The back of the brain is where we react before we think about what we are doing.*

For example:

This is why we run away from a fire instead of running into the fire. It tries to keep us from danger. Sometimes, the back of the brain, gets overworked and fires off waaay too much, especially when we are

angry,   mad,   scared,   or...

don't want to do what we are supposed to do. *

When that happens our brain gets STUCK.

I've reacted without thinking, like when I get mad at someone and say something I shouldn't say. Instead, we need to SHIFT and use the front of our brain.

11

The front of the brain is where we are

thinkers,

problem solvers,

and learners.

We want to use this
part of our brain
the most.
This makes
our brain stronger.

I want to use the front of my brain.
I bet you want to too.

Here are two REMINDERS that help me use the front of my brain and help me become a better thinker.

1. CHECK

2. CRISSCROSS and SHIFT

These REMINDERS help me learn to SHIFT to the front of my brain instead of being STUCK in the back of my brain.

This is why I'm sharing them with you.

Check

Crisscross and Shift

First, let's talk about CHECK.

When an adult says **CHECK** to me, I know I need to change my behavior.

I think about what I am doing that needs to stop.
Then, I change my behavior to do the right thing.
That way, I'm doing the thinking.
It's my brain that tells me what to do.
And it's my brain that gets stronger in the front.
The adult is just giving me a reminder.

When I am **CHECKED**, I take care of it right away.
And when someone says **CHECK** to you, you'll take care of it right away too.*

14

The second way I help my brain is called CRISS-CROSS and SHIFT.

When an adult asks me to CRISSCROSS and SHIFT, or they might say SHIFT, I do a brain-building activity that looks like this.*

Let's see you do it.

You sit **CRISSCROSS** with your legs and then **CRISSCROSS** your arms.

Make sure that if your right leg goes over your left leg then your left arm needs to go over your right arm and vice versa.*

This **CRISSCROSSING** activates both sides of your brain and helps your brain **SHIFT** to the front.

Wow! What a good job you're doing!

CRISSCROSSING and SHIFTING also gets oxygen to your brain which helps your brain. But you have to sit up tall and straight, breathe slowly without talking.

You can CRISSCROSS like this for a few minutes until you have SHIFTED and are ready to be a good thinker.

And when an adult asks you what happened, you will be able to give a good answer. *

oxygen

I give a good answer after I CRISSCROSS and SHIFT.
You will too.

You can also **CRISSCROSS** if you are crying, mad, angry, upset, wanting to calm down, or trying to be a better thinker.

The important thing is to **CRISSCROSS** right away so you don't get **STUCK** in the back of the brain.

So, I **CRISSCROSS** and **SHIFT** right away when an adult tells me.

Sometimes I do it all on my own when I need to. I know it is good for me.

It's good for you too!

Here are some rules that go with these reminders:

- Only an adult tells someone to **CHECK** and/or **CRISSCROSS** and **SHIFT**.

- When told to **CHECK** and/or **CRISSCROSS** and **SHIFT**, do it right away.

- You may **CHECK** and/or **CRISSCROSS** and **SHIFT** anytime you think it will help you be a better thinker.

Our brain is extremely important!
It's the only one we have!
So we need to take care of it.
I'm taking care of my brain.
Are you taking care of yours?

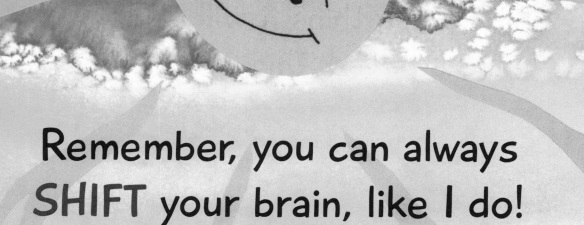

Remember, you can always
SHIFT your brain, like I do!

TIPS FOR USING THIS RESOURCE

Page 4

Merriam Wester defines an organ as a part of the body that has a particular function. We rarely think of the brain as an organ. So, it is important that children know it is an organ.

Page 6

Many examples of protection would be: bike helmets, motorcycle helmet, sports helmet, horseback helmet, seatbelt.

Page 7

Here is a great chance to have a discussion on healthy foods, good thoughts, what we put in or receive in our brain: television, play, games, music, drugs etc.

Page 10

The fight/flight response is often described as a reaction that occurs in the primal brain. This is a where we react if threatened, frightened, or scared, etc. It is designed to ensure our survival.

Page 11

It is good for children to connect their reactions to their responses. I often ask a child, "Were you reacting or thinking?"

Page 11

Remind children that it is okay to have feelings. Angry, mad, scared, etc. are all feelings. It is how we handle our feelings that is important. We can have these feelings but it would be wrong if we let this feelings react in a way that we hurt ourselves or someone else.

Page 14

CHECK: Do a few role plays to show children what is meant by check. For example: If someone is tipping their chair, you say, "check", they quickly stop tipping the chair. When you say, "check" to a child that has interrupted you, they should stop. If a child starts to beg for something, you say "check" to them. After a child takes care of the behavior, say to them, "Good thinking."

Pages 15-16

CRISSCOSS and SHIFT: Be very specific about the way a child does this brain-building activity. It is important that they sit up straight and breathe slowly, getting oxygen to their brain. Do not allow a sloppy sit or talking. They must be silent to shift and be thinking about what they have done or what they are going to do. Children need to practice this brain-building activity in order to build up their time to sit longer. They can start with just sitting for one minute. Eventually, they should be able to do this crisscross for at least a minute per year of age.

A younger child can simply cross her arms over her chest.

Here are some examples of when and how to use crisscross and shift.

1. Lying - "I notice that the flower vase on my counter is cracked. So before we talk about this, show me a really good crisscross. Remember to shift and be a good thinker so we can discuss this when you're ready."

2. Crying - child crying over a toy that broke. "I can see that you're crying and upset so, do a crisscross, shift and think about what needs to be done. When you're ready we can talk about it."

3. Not Listening - "I have told you to get ready for school and I can see that you're still in your pajamas. Do a crisscross and think about what you should be doing. When you're ready you can tell me what you're going to do."

Being a good thinker:
After a child has crisscrossed and shifted, ask them, "What happened? Why did you do a crisscross?" This is when you can process with your child. They can also crisscross to be thinking ahead about how they will behave before going somewhere. After they have crisscrossed, have them tell you how they will behave.

Crisscrossing should be introduced as a positive activity that is helping their brain, rather than a negative activity or punishment. Examples for positive times:
Before watching a special program on TV
When they have finished getting ready for bed (waiting for you to read a book)
Before going somewhere (they could think about how they will behave when you go to the grocery store, shopping, movie theater etc.)

Older children can crisscross in a sitting position on the floor.

Make sure children are doing opposite crossing.

Older children can also crisscross sitting in a chair.

Other brain-building activities include:
• Jumping Jacks
• Jumping on a Trampoline
• Running
• Swinging

LOOK FOR THESE AND OTHER RELATED RESOURCES FROM

yl@youthlightbooks.com   youth light inc.   www.youthlight.com

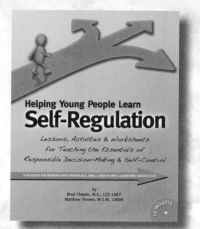

Helping Young People Learn Self-Regulation

Lessons, Activities and Worksheets for Teaching the Essentials of Responsible Decision-Making & Self-Control (includes a CD-ROM of reproducible worksheets)

By: Brad Chapin, MS, LCP, LMLP and Matthew Penner

Self-regulation includes a universal set of skills necessary for academic success emotional control and healthy social interaction. With this single resource you will be able to address children's anger problems academic performance challenges anxieties school safety issues self-esteem social skills and much more.

These strategies in this resource can be used individually for a quick intervention with children. They can also be used to create dozens of unique curricula tailor-made to target specific problem areas for small groups or classrooms.

As the term 'self-regulation' suggests, this approach focuses on teaching children how to regulate their own emotions and behaviors. The authors have split the self-regulation training process into three functional area: physical emotional and cognitive. Using strategies based soundly upon the evidence base of cognitive-behavioral psychology this resource will help you move children progressively through skill areas in each of these three domains.

"SMART" Guidance: Teaching Self-Regulation to Children Through Interactive Lessons

By: Will Moody & Brad Chapin

Unique Interactive Lessons Designed for Use on Windows and MAC-Based Workstations and Digital Whiteboards such as SMART Boards and Promethean Boards.

Self-Regulation Training Board

By: Brad Chapin, MS, LCP, LMLP

The Self-Regulation Training Board is a great tool for any classroom, office or home. It provides a very concrete, practical way for children to learn and practice their Self-Regulation skills. The 11 X 17 Board and the moveable pieces are laminated. It can easily be pinned up in an office, designated area of the classroom or home.

This tool reinforces the Self-Regulation Training framework. When processing a situation, children are able to mark where they felt their Physical Warning Signs on the green person. Next, they are able to place an Emotion in the box to indicate how they Feel. Finally, they can choose a skill they've learned to indicate how they will solve the issue.

These highly interactive lessons are designed to teach students the skills, strategies, and behaviors they need to regulate their own physical, emotional, and cognitive processes.

- Melting Freeze (Regulate BODY)
- Animal Movements (Regulate BODY)
- Cooling the Flame (Regulate BODY)
- Name Your Emotions (Regulate EMOTIONS)
- Emotional Rain Gauge (Regulate EMOTIONS)
- Emotional Knot (Regulate EMOTIONS)
- Don't Take the Bait (Regulate THOUGHTS)
- Defiance Trap (Regulate THOUGHTS)
- Domino Effect (Regulate THOUGHTS)
- Magnetic Thoughts (Regulate THOUGHTS)

LOOK FOR THESE AND OTHER RELATED RESOURCES FROM

yl@youthlightbooks.com   www.youthlight.com

Big Deals and Little Deals and What to Do When They Happen to You

Problem-Solving Skills for Children Grades PK-4
(includes a CD-ROM with animated storybook, interactive lessons, posters and more)

By: Kim Edmister

At long last, simple and clear-cut guidelines for helping children differentiate big deals - situations that require adult intervention and little deals - those things children are capable of handling on their own. Eliminate the need to give constant reminders to "Stop tattling." Instead, empower children by prompting, "Is it a big deal or a little deal?" Once they have learned the difference and know the strategies, they are better equipped to cope with and handle life's everyday difficulties independently.

BONUS CD!!! This resource includes a CD with the story in an interactive format along with additional interactive lessons to use on your interactive whiteboards such as SMART Board™ or Promothean Board™. It also includes 11 posters in pdf format that you can print and display, tent signs for the students' desks to remind them of the strategies to handle little deals on their own, song lyrics sung to the tune of "Itsy Bitsy Spider" and other reproducible worksheets.

The Big Red Bird & Red Feather Game

A Book About Calming and Self-Control Skills for Children When They are Upset

By: Cindy Wetzel

The Big Red Bird is a caring, delightful feathered friend. In this story, she becomes very upset after she notices some children yelling, arguing and name-calling at one another. Luckily she knew a wonderful skill to help herself calm down so she could think better about doing the right thing. She then teaches the children how to use this skill using some of her red feathers.

This book provides a fun, unforgettable way children can improve their self-regulation when they are upset, or feel an urge to act out. It is a valuable resource for children who have difficulties with impulse control.

Included are several worksheets at the end to reinforce the lesson. The book also includes game instructions and a package with some real red feathers for "The Red Feather Game." This can be played by one or more children and will enhance the techniques learned from the story.

Challenge Software DVD

Video Clips, Discussion Questions and Follow-Up Activities

By: Brad Chapin

The Challenge Software DVD is based upon an internet-based Challenge Software solution. This interactive tool is designed to help students in grades K-8 to improve their self-regulation insights and skills. It is intended to be used on any personal computer that has DVD-playing capability. This program provides an unforgettable, fun way to build impulse-control capabilities is students.

This interactive program presents 17 brief, posterized video clips showing common scenarios in the lives of young people. An individual or small group (or a classroom of students if using SMART technology) would watch one of the scenarios until it reaches a decision point. The individual or group is then asked to choose between several ways that the main character could think about the event that just took place. After making a choice and watching its outcome, the observer(s) can then choose to view the outcome of an alternate decision. While the scenarios are based upon the internet-based Challenge Software, the DVD does not offer tracking capability or decision-based branching.